James Madison

Father of the Constitution

Colonial Leaders

Lord Baltimore
English Politician and Colonist

Benjamin Banneker
American Mathematician and Astronomer

Sir William Berkeley
Governor of Virginia

William Bradford
Governor of Plymouth Colony

Jonathan Edwards
Colonial Religious Leader

Benjamin Franklin
American Statesman, Scientist, and Writer

Anne Hutchinson
Religious Leader

Cotton Mather
Author, Clergyman, and Scholar

Increase Mather
Clergyman and Scholar

James Oglethorpe
Humanitarian and Soldier

William Penn
Founder of Democracy

Sir Walter Raleigh
English Explorer and Author

Caesar Rodney
American Patriot

John Smith
English Explorer and Colonist

Miles Standish
Plymouth Colony Leader

Peter Stuyvesant
Dutch Military Leader

George Whitefield
Clergyman and Scholar

Roger Williams
Founder of Rhode Island

John Winthrop
Politician and Statesman

John Peter Zenger
Free Press Advocate

Revolutionary War Leaders

John Adams
Second U.S. President

Ethan Allen
Revolutionary Hero

Benedict Arnold
Traitor to the Cause

King George III
English Monarch

Nathanael Greene
Military Leader

Nathan Hale
Revolutionary Hero

Alexander Hamilton
First U.S. Secretary of the Treasury

John Hancock
President of the Continental Congress

Patrick Henry
American Statesman and Speaker

John Jay
First Chief Justice of the Supreme Court

Thomas Jefferson
Author of the Declaration of Independence

John Paul Jones
Father of the U.S. Navy

Lafayette
French Freedom Fighter

James Madison
Father of the Constitution

Francis Marion
The Swamp Fox

James Monroe
American Statesman

Thomas Paine
Political Writer

Paul Revere
American Patriot

Betsy Ross
American Patriot

George Washington
First U.S. President

Famous Figures of the Civil War Era

Jefferson Davis
Confederate President

Frederick Douglass
Abolitionist and Author

Ulysses S. Grant
Military Leader and President

Stonewall Jackson
Confederate General

Robert E. Lee
Confederate General

Abraham Lincoln
Civil War President

William Sherman
Union General

Harriet Beecher Stowe
Author of Uncle Tom's Cabin

Sojourner Truth
Abolitionist, Suffragist, and Preacher

Harriet Tubman
Leader of the Underground Railroad

Revolutionary War Leaders

James Madison

Father of the Constitution

Brent Kelley

Arthur M. Schlesinger, jr.
Senior Consulting Editor

Chelsea House Publishers

Philadelphia

Produced by 21st Century Publishing and Communications, Inc.
New York, NY. http://www.21cpc.com

CHELSEA HOUSE PUBLISHERS
Production Manager Pamela Loos
Art Director Sara Davis
Director of Photography Judy L. Hasday
Managing Editor James D. Gallagher
Senior Production Editor J. Christopher Higgins

Staff for *JAMES MADISON*
Project Editor/Publishing Coordinator Jim McAvoy
Project Editor Anne Hill
Associate Art Director Takeshi Takahashi
Series Design Keith Trego

The Chelsea House World Wide Web address is
http://www.chelseahouse.com

First Printing
1 3 5 7 9 8 6 4 2

Library of Congress Cataloging-in-Publication Data

Kelley, Brent P.
James Madison / by Brent Kelley.
    p.   cm. — (Revolutionary War leaders)
Includes bibliographical references (p.   ) and index.
Summary: A biography of the "Father of the Constitution" and fourth
president of the United States.
ISBN 0-7910-5972-3 (hc) — 0-7910-6130-2 (pbk.)
1. Madison, James, 1751-1836—Juvenile literature. 2. Presidents—
United States—Biography—Juvenile literature. 3. United States—
History—Revolution, 1775-1783—Biography—Juvenile literature.
4. United States—History—War of 1812—Juvenile literature. 5. United
States—Politics and government—1809-1817—Juvenile literature.
[1. Madison, James, 1751-1836. 2. Presidents.] I. Title. II. Series.
E342.K38   2000
973.5'1'092—dc21
[B]   00-026853
                                                               CIP

Publisher's Note: In Colonial and Revolutionary War America,
there were no standard rules for spelling, punctuation, capitaliza-
tion, or grammar. Some of the quotations that appear in the Colonial Leaders and Revolutionary War Leaders series come from
original documents and letters written during this time in history.
Original quotations reflect writing inconsistencies of the period.

Contents

James Madison grew up in a big house on a plantation in Virginia. The Madisons were a very wealthy family with many servants.

Early Years

When James Madison was born on March 5, 1750, no one was sure he would live. Many babies died before they were a year old in those days. James was not very strong. His parents, James and Nelly Conway Madison, did everything they could to take care of him.

In time, the Madisons had 11 more children. Five of them died while they were very young. Their big brother James almost died too. He was always small, pale, and sickly. He wasn't strong enough to speak in a loud voice. He got tired easily and had little energy.

James was born in Port Conway, Virginia, at the

home of his mother's parents. Very soon, mother and son returned to the family plantation in Orange County, Virginia.

This plantation was very large–5,000 acres. The Madisons grew tobacco and grain. The work was done by about 100 slaves. The Madisons were a wealthy family.

Shortly after James was born, the date of his birthday changed. The earth travels around the sun about once a year. It actually takes a little longer than a year. So every four years we add an extra day to the year, which is called leap year. But the calendars used by the American colonies didn't have leap years. By the time James was born the calendar had fallen more than a year behind.

The Madison plantation was huge. It was much too big for one family to take care of. Hired farm help was expensive and hard to find. Like most plantation owners, the Madisons used slaves.

When James Madison was very young, he didn't understand that the black workers on the plantation were "owned" by his family. Once he learned the truth, he did not approve. Throughout his life he was against slavery, but he kept slaves at his home. Unlike many slave owners, he let families of slaves stay together.

Slaves working in the fields on the plantation. James did not like the idea of slavery–that people could be owned by another person.

To catch up, people added all those missing days to the calendar and then started using leap years. Everyone's birthday changed to fit the new calendar. James's birthday was now March 16, 1751.

James was called "Jemmy" by his family. Jemmy didn't have much work to do because slaves did all the chores. And with so many brothers and sisters, plus the children of all the

Children's books were very rare in the 1700s. The Madisons didn't have any. The books they did have were all written by adults for adults. Nine-year-old Jemmy liked them anyway. If he didn't understand something in one of them, he could ask his father about it, and he often did.

One book should have been interesting to Jemmy because of his health problems. It was a book on childhood diseases. Another was on bathing in cold water. The author claimed it was healthy. One book was titled *The Employment of the Microscope*, and it made Jemmy want one.

slaves, there were plenty of playmates. But Jemmy often preferred to read by himself.

Jemmy loved the trees on the plantation. There were two tulip poplars called "The Twins," and a grove of walnut trees that made the perfect place to sit and read. His favorite trees were the redbuds. He loved their bright pink blossoms in the spring.

Jemmy asked a lot of questions. That was one reason he read so much. He found answers in books. By the time he turned 11, he had read all 85 of his father's books. He had read some of them twice.

Jemmy asked his father for more books. Rather than buy more books, Mr. Madison decided to

James loved reading books, so his father sent him to a school like this one. There he studied English, French, Latin, and Greek.

send his son to school. So 11-year-old Jemmy was sent to a small school in a nearby county.

The school had dozens of books, and James, as he was now called, read all the ones that were written in English. Then he learned French, Latin, and Greek so he could also read the books written in those languages.

James's teacher taught him history, algebra, geometry, and astronomy. Astronomy was one of James's favorite subjects.

James remained at the school for five years. He loved it. He wanted to stay longer, but when he was 16 his father brought him home. James had a new teacher. Mr. Martin was a minister who lived with the Madisons. One of Mr. Martin's jobs was to prepare James for college.

In those days, most young men from Virginia who attended college went to the College of William and Mary in Williamsburg. Mr. Madison did not like what he heard about that school. People said that the students were too rowdy and drank too much.

Mr. Madison thought James needed more serious classmates. He decided James would go to the College of New Jersey (now called Princeton University).

At the age of 18, James set out on horseback for the long ride to New Jersey. Mr. Martin traveled with him. Even though James was slightly older than most of the other students, he looked much younger. He stood barely 5' 3" tall and weighed about 90 pounds. He could easily have been mistaken for being only 13 or 14 years old.

Because James was always sick, going far away from home was a brave thing to do. He suffered from fevers. One doctor said he had "liver distress."

Now and then, James also had seizures. He would become rigid for a few minutes and be unable to speak. One doctor said the illness was a nervous disorder. Another doctor said it was probably **epilepsy.** James called it simply "falling sickness" because that's what it made him do. All his life, James tended to worry about getting sick.

When he arrived at the College of New Jersey, James found out that he knew more than other freshmen, or first-year students. He met with college officials and they decided to admit him as a sophomore, or second-year student. Books were everywhere. James knew he would love college.

James read a great deal and studied hard while at the College of New Jersey at Princeton, but he also had fun with his new friends.

2

College Life

James found life at the College of New Jersey very exciting. He had a lot of fun that first year.

Pranks were played just as they are in colleges today, though some of them would now be seen as serious. The students set off firecrackers in the rooms of other new students, or they placed greasy feathers on floors where people would slip on them.

For James, the best part of college was the library. There, he found more books than he ever imagined could be in one place. He read as often as he could. He read books about everything. His favorite books were about **theology**, law, and history.

Most of the students were interested in politics. They read everything they could about Britain and the American colonies. Many students were upset about the taxes the British were **levying** on the colonies.

American merchants wanted to do something that would show Britain how much they hated the taxes. They agreed to stop buying goods from Britain. The students thought this agreement was a great idea. But in 1770, New York merchants decided to break the agreement. When the students at the College of New Jersey heard about this, they demonstrated by marching across the campus and ringing all the bells. James joined right in. It was the first time he had ever been caught up in politics.

James's best friend at school was a young man named Joe Ross. Joe was as good a student and as **avid** a reader as James. They both loved school, but they made a plan to complete their last two years in only one year. They needed to get permission from the college's president to

**James loved his time at college and was
a good student. He also learned more
about, and found purpose in, the colonies'
political struggle with Great Britain.**

do this. They convinced him that they were up
to the challenge.

James and Joe worked very hard to complete

two years of study in just one year. They slept only five hours a night. The lack of sleep wasn't good for either of them. James became very ill. But he still got his schoolwork done on time.

Eleven students graduated from the College of New Jersey in 1771. But only 10 were able to attend the ceremonies. James was absent from his graduation because he was too sick to go. Joe was sick, too, but he was well enough to attend the big event. The 10 graduates present gave speeches. One member of the class received an award for his good spelling. That person was Aaron Burr, who would later introduce James to his future wife, Dolley.

James really had no plans for what he was going to do after he graduated. Most of the students planned to become lawyers or ministers. James did not feel he was suited for either type of work.

If he had been able to, he probably would have become a preacher. But a preacher had to speak loudly to deliver his sermons. James could not do this. His voice had always been soft, and shouting was impossible for him.

The same problem stopped him from being a lawyer. A lawyer needed to speak up to argue a case in court. James didn't really want to be a lawyer anyway.

The young graduate was so sick when school ended that he could not make the long trip home to Virginia, so he stayed at the college. James was no longer a student, but he wanted to keep learning. With the help of the college president James studied theology, as well as Hebrew. Slowly, his health improved.

Mr. Madison decided that he wanted James at home to teach his younger brothers and sisters. He sent for the young man in April 1772. It was not a request. It was an order.

The trip from college to the Madisons' plantation took a whole week by horseback. Riding a horse for many hours a day was hard work. James still wasn't feeling well. By the time he got home, he was very sick again.

Still, James taught his younger brothers and

When James was a young man, the usual mode of transportation was by horse. It took a week to ride from his college in New Jersey to his home in Virginia.

sisters for a few hours each day. He read as often as he could. But most of the time he just sat around because he was very tired.

James didn't seem interested in anything. Even the conflicts between Britain and the colonies didn't get him excited. He wrote to a friend, "I do not meddle in Politicks."

One day, James received a letter. It said that his best friend from college, Joe Ross, had died. James took this news very hard. He became very sad. He blamed Joe's death on all the hard work they had done at school. James thought that he might die young, too.

His father was very worried about James. The boy seemed to get worse every week. Finally, James's father sent him to a health resort. It had mineral waters that were supposed to cure many illnesses. But James returned home no better than when he left.

Late in December 1773, a friend from college wrote James a letter. He told James about a group of colonists in Boston who were so angry about British taxes they dumped British tea into the harbor. James was excited to learn of this event, which became known as the Boston Tea Party.

Slowly, James began showing signs of life. He stopped feeling so sad and things began to interest him again.

In 1774 he was healthy enough to travel with

his brother William to the College of New Jersey. William was also going to attend the school. When they passed through Philadelphia, James saw that a group of men from all the colonies were meeting there. This was a meeting of the first Continental Congress.

James was so interested in all that was happening that he decided to become involved in politics, too. He wanted to vote. That way he could have a say in what happened. But only men who owned land could vote. In the fall of that year, James purchased 200 acres from his father so he could vote and even hold public office.

In December 1774, James did just that. Both he and his father were elected to serve on the Orange County Committee of Safety. The committee had two main jobs. It was to make sure that all of the county's residents were prepared to fight if war broke out. It was also supposed to see that all of the county's residents were loyal to Virginia and not to the British.

Philadelphia, the meeting place of the Continental Congress. During a short visit there, James became interested in colonial politics.

People who were disloyal to the American colonies were called Tories. Anyone who was a Tory received a terrible punishment. Some people were coated with hot tar. Then they were covered with feathers and marched through the streets. Others were shot and killed. No one was forgiven for being loyal to Great Britain instead

Men could serve on political committees like this one only if they were landowners. Because of this rule, James bought land and became a voter.

of to Virginia.

James hated Tories. He said that if the other colonies had a problem with punishing Tories, they should send them to Orange County.

James wanted to become a soldier, but he couldn't because of his "falling sickness." No one wanted a soldier who would fall down in the middle of a battle. He joined the local **militia** and was given the rank of colonel. But the work was too hard for him. On the very first day of drills, he passed out.

Even this did not slow him down. James was determined and kept on trying. In a short time, he became an excellent marksman. He could hit his target from 100 yards away.

But James lost his desire to be a soldier when he realized he could fight in another way. He could fight for the American colonies by helping to make decisions about what should be done. James set a new goal for himself. He was going to become more involved in politics.

In colonial times, Williamsburg was the capital of Virginia. As a delegate to the 1776 state convention there, James joined a committee to write the state constitution.

3

"The Father of the Constitution"

In May 1776, James was elected the representative from Orange County, Virginia, to a state convention in Williamsburg. He was 25 years old and firmly hooked on politics.

At the convention, James listened to people talk about the Continental Congress. Men representing the American colonies were meeting in Philadelphia and deciding what to do about problems with Great Britain.

The Virginia state convention decided to send a message to their representatives in Philadelphia. The Virginia representatives were told to propose a

Declaration of Independence from Great Britain.

James was put on the committee to write a **constitution** for Virginia. His job was to come up with a list of "**inalienable rights**." These are freedoms that cannot be kept or taken away from the citizens. As the meetings went on, James was very quiet. The only times he spoke were when he whispered his thoughts and comments to his friend Edmund Randolph.

After the state convention ended, James wanted another political office. He ran for the Virginia House of Delegates, the new **legislature** of the colony. Voters knew and liked James. He didn't like **campaigning**, and he was so certain that he would win that he did little work to convince people to vote for him.

James's opponent was an older, more experienced politician, who knew how to get elected. He set up a barrel of whisky outside the courthouse where the voting took place and gave each person who came to vote a drink. James lost.

Discouraged, James went home. A short time later, the House of Delegates elected him to fill a spot in the Council of State. This eight-man group decided important matters for Virginia. The head was the governor of Virginia, Patrick Henry.

Another member of the Council of State was a 32-year-old lawyer named Thomas Jefferson. James and Thomas found they had much in common. They both loved horses, the land, and literature. Also, they both were strongly in favor of freedom of religion, and they both intensely disliked Governor Henry.

The two men soon became best friends even though they looked and acted very differently from each other. Thomas was a tall, red-headed, outgoing married man. James was a very short, dark-haired, soft-spoken bachelor. But they worked very well together.

Patrick Henry almost always disagreed with James and Thomas. If they supported something, Governor Henry was against it. The governor gave powerful speeches. He once gave a speech

Patrick Henry, governor of Virginia, always seemed to disagree with James's ideas about politics.

against one of James and Thomas's ideas.

James turned to Thomas and asked, "What shall we do with him?"

Thomas replied, "What we have to do, I think, is devoutly pray for his death."

But in spite of Governor Henry's opposition, the council agreed with many of James and Thomas's ideas. They got many things done. The two friends became well known.

In December 1779, James was elected a delegate to the Continental Congress in Philadelphia. He was very excited–he had wanted this job for a long time. He was supposed to go to Philadelphia immediately. But on the day he was going to leave, it snowed heavily. The entire East Coast eventually suffered one of the worst winters ever. No one could travel for weeks. James couldn't get to Philadelphia

While in Philadelphia for the Continental Congress, James lived in a house with several other people, one of whom was a pretty, 16-year-old girl named Kitty Floyd. Kitty was there with her father, a New York delegate. James was 32 years old, but he courted her anyway.

In early spring of 1783, James asked Kitty to marry him. She said yes. But in April she went home to New York with her father. In July, she wrote James that she had changed her mind. James was heartbroken.

until March 18, 1780.

As a newcomer to the city, James was invited to many parties so the people could meet him. Quiet as always, he didn't make much of an impression. One important woman in Philadelphia society described him as gloomy and stiff.

As usual, James sat quietly through the meetings of the Continental Congress. Its members were debating a new constitution, called the Articles of Confederation. James thought the Articles wouldn't work. He felt that they didn't create a Congress with enough power to be effective.

The Revolutionary War continued as James and the other men tried to agree about what path the country should take. Reports from the battlefields arrived in Philadelphia. Many of them were not good.

The British had captured some of the members of the Virginia House of Delegates. They almost caught Thomas Jefferson. James's plantation home, which he now called Montpelier, was also in danger. But he was far away and knew nothing about this threat until several weeks later.

Soon thereafter, the Americans began to win some key battles. Then, on October 19, 1781, British general Charles Cornwallis surrendered to George Washington at Yorktown, Virginia. Two years later, with the signing of a peace treaty in Paris, the war was over. America had won.

After four years as a delegate in Philadelphia, James returned to Montpelier. In 1784, he was elected to the Virginia House of Delegates. Richmond had become the capital of Virginia, and Patrick Henry was still against whatever James was for.

In 1785, someone suggested that representatives from Maryland and Virginia meet to discuss **navigation** problems on the Potomac River, which runs between the two states.

The Virginia House of Delegates did not meet in the summer of 1784. At that time James met the Marquis de Lafayette in Baltimore, who told James he was going to travel up New York's Hudson River to sign an Indian treaty.

James was invited along. The two men took a barge as far as Albany, and then went on foot through the woods.

James loved the adventure. The trip took so long that he returned late for the fall session. He had to pay a fine to the House of Delegates for being late. But he did not mind because he had such a good time.

James and his friend Edmund Randolph were among the delegates from Virginia. Governor Henry didn't tell them when the meeting was to be held. So they missed it. At the meeting it was decided that representatives from the two states should meet each year. But when James heard this he suggested that delegates from all 13 states should meet to discuss how to govern the new nation.

This meeting was held the first Monday of September 1786, in Annapolis, Maryland. Only 12 men showed up. Massachusetts sent no one, and several states sent only one person. Those 12 delegates who came planned a new convention, asking Congress to request proper representation from all states. The meeting was set for May 14, 1787, in Philadelphia.

This time, all the states except Rhode Island sent representatives. Most of them arrived late. James arrived on May 3, but it was May 25 before enough men were present to do anything. The meeting would eventually be known as the Constitutional Convention.

James wanted the Articles of Confederation changed. He thought they were too weak. He wanted to scrap them and replace them with a brand new constitution. But James knew that his weak voice and small size were a problem. He was afraid that no one would take his ideas seriously if he presented them. So he had his friend Edmund Randolph propose his ideas. Edmund was tall, handsome, and a good speaker. James was sure Randolph would impress the other men.

And Randolph did. With James's guidance, he suggested a form of government that would have more power over the states. Randolph proposed a strong national government with a new constitution. This came to be known as the Virginia Plan.

The plan called for three branches of the national government: the executive branch (the president); the judicial branch (the courts); and the legislative branch (a Senate and a House of Representatives).

Once Edmund Randolph gave his speech,

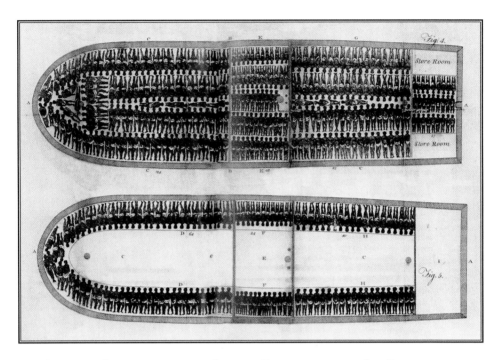

A ship used to transport slaves. James wanted a law to stop the slave trade, but pressure from the Southern states forced a compromise.

the men began debating. Many of them had to be convinced that this plan was best for the nation. Some were slow to agree.

William Paterson of New Jersey wanted to keep the Articles of Confederation. This idea became known as the New Jersey Plan.

James also wanted the new nation to outlaw the slave trade. The representatives from Georgia and South Carolina threatened to leave the Union if the slave trade ended. A compromise was reached. The men agreed that the slave trade could not be done away with before 1808. This would not stop slavery. It simply stopped people from bringing new slaves to America from Africa.

The Constitution was finally completed on September 17, 1787. Everyone had helped with the final document, but they knew it was mostly the work and ideas of James Madison.

Even though the Constitution had been written, it was a long way from being put into effect. Each state had to **ratify**, or vote to accept, the new Constitution. Nine of the 13 states had to approve it before it became law.

More problems arose. Many people didn't understand the Constitution. A chief executive sounded too much like a king to them. They had just fought to have a country without a king.

To many Americans, the national government looked as if it would be too strong. It might take away all the powers of the states. And a big problem for many was that the document did not list citizens' inalienable rights. The people had to be convinced that the Constitution was a good thing.

James Madison, Alexander Hamilton, and John Jay decided to do the convincing. The three men wrote 85 letters that appeared in a New York newspaper. They used the **pen name** "Publius." These letters were later published as a book called *The Federalist Papers*. Because of these letters, many more people began to understand the importance of ratifying the Constitution.

The ratifying conventions in each state took place from 1787 to 1788. Six states—Delaware, New Jersey, Georgia, Connecticut, Maryland, and South Carolina—quickly voted yes. Pennsylvania debated long and hard. In time, it also voted to ratify the Constitution. Massachusetts took a month of debate before it voted in favor of it. That was eight of the nine states needed.

But three states probably wouldn't accept the new Constitution. They were New York, North Carolina, and Rhode Island. And no one knew which way New Hampshire would go.

James and the Virginia delegation met in Richmond. Patrick Henry was completely against the idea of the Constitution. For two days, he and his followers spoke against it. James had Edmund Randolph try to answer their speeches, but it didn't help much. The debating took a lot out of James. He became sick and spent the next four days in bed. But he had good friends who defended the Constitution when he was too sick to do so.

At last, on June 6, 1788, the Virginia delegates voted. Patrick Henry gave one last speech against the Constitution. It didn't work. James and his supporters won. Virginia ratified the Constitution by a vote of 89 to 79.

James was very happy. He thought that his home state of Virginia was the ninth state to ratify the Constitution. Now that nine states had voted in its favor, the Constitution was the law of the land.

Word came later that New Hampshire had actually agreed to ratify the Constitution a few days earlier than Virginia. That did not make James any less happy. In July, New York also voted to adopt the Constitution, but Rhode Island and North Carolina did not.

For all of his work, James became known as "the Father of the Constitution."

The next order of business for the United States was the election of the first president and vice president. At that time, the man who received the most votes became president. The man who came in second became vice president. George Washington won, and John Adams of Massachusetts received the second highest number of votes.

James wanted to be a senator. At that time, senators were chosen by their state legislatures. Patrick Henry controlled the Virginia legislature. He did not like James. He made sure that James did not become a senator.

So James ran for the House of Representatives. Again, Governor Henry tried to keep James from winning the election. But James gave speeches

George Washington, the first president of the United States, arrives in New York. James wrote many of Washington's important speeches.

and met with the voters. He didn't like speaking in public, but he won the election easily.

As George Washington's presidential **inauguration** neared, he showed James the speech he would be giving. James did not like it. It was too long. So James rewrote the speech for Washington.

Later, when President Washington was to give a speech to the House of Representatives in New York City, James wrote that, too. When it came time for the House to reply to the president's speech, James also wrote that. Then Washington had to answer the reply. James wrote that for the president. He was very busy writing speeches.

That first session of the House of Representatives was confusing. After all, it was the first House of Representatives. The new representatives had no **precedents** set for them. James wrote to his father, saying, "We are in a wilderness without a single footstep to guide us."

As the session went on, things began to run more smoothly. And as the representatives settled in, things began to get accomplished. **Cabinet** posts were created. A national court system was built. Both of these ideas came from James.

Then James proposed 10 **amendments**, or changes, to the Constitution. The 10 amendments were called the Bill of Rights. They described the rights and freedoms guaranteed to U.S. citizens.

James served in the first House of Representatives, which met in 1789 in New York City.

Some men didn't like this idea.

The biggest problem was how the amendment promising freedom of religion would be worded. This amendment was very important to James. It took four months to get the wording just right.

Then the Bill of Rights had to be ratified just as the Constitution had been. That took more than a year. In December 1791, the Bill of Rights was ratified and added to the Constitution.

The year before, Congress had authorized building the nation's capital beside the Potomac River. This was the place where James had wanted it to be. Even that decision took a while to make. Many men suggested other locations. James kept reminding them that none of the other places would work as well as the land along the river. It became Washington, D.C.

The next problem was one James had never expected. His old friend and **ally** Alexander Hamilton served in the president's cabinet. He was the secretary of the treasury. Hamilton came up with a plan to pay the national debt.

James, along with Thomas Jefferson, believed Hamilton's plan helped the rich and hurt other people. James and Thomas felt the debt should be paid by everyone. They didn't think that poor people should pay most of the bills.

They solved this problem, but in the process James and Hamilton drifted apart. They were no longer good friends. James Madison, Thomas

Jefferson, and Alexander Hamilton still agreed about some things though. One belief they shared was that George Washington should be president for another term. President Washington wanted to retire. He had asked James to write a farewell speech for him. In the end, the three men were able to convince the president to stay in office.

New problems came up. In 1789 the French Revolution had taken place in France. By 1792 the king of France and many other people had been killed. A new government was formed, and it was trying to start revolutions in other nations.

France had helped the American colonies fight against Great Britain in the Revolutionary War. Many people in the United States wanted to help France in its wars.

Great Britain and France had been enemies for many years. The British government did not want a lot of wars in Europe. The British asked the Americans to help them keep the French from starting wars. President Washington said the United States wouldn't take sides.

After the French Revolution, Congress debated about whether to help America's old ally, France, or to side with Great Britain.

The men in Congress debated over what should be done next. People did not agree. Once again, James and Hamilton were at odds. Those who followed Hamilton's ideas called themselves "Federalists." Those who agreed with James and his friend Jefferson called themselves "Republicans."

Even though President Washington said the United States wouldn't take sides, people still argued about the subject. The Federalists wanted to help Great Britain. But the Republicans remembered France's **alliance** with the colonies during the Revolutionary War. They wanted to be on the side of the French. The entire nation was upset over this.

James was sad. Because he disagreed with Hamilton and Washington, they were no longer good friends. He was 43 years old and he thought he might leave politics. But before he quit, he would finish his job. He didn't want to disappoint the people of Virginia.

Meanwhile, temporarily, the national government moved to Philadelphia, until the new capital could be planned and built. The House of Representatives met in Philadelphia in the fall of 1793. That summer a disease called yellow fever had swept through the city. About 4,000 people had died from the disease and the city

James's wife Dolley Madison, who later became one of America's most popular first ladies.

was trying to recover. Among those who died were a young lawyer named John Todd and his infant son. Todd left a widow, Dolley Payne

Todd, and a one-year-old son named Payne. (Many history books say her name was "Dorothea." Some spell her name "Dolly." But "Dolley" was the name her parents gave her.)

Dolley was a pretty, outgoing, 25-year-old woman. She took good care of her family and business matters. In case something happened to her, she named a family friend, Aaron Burr, to take care of little Payne. Burr and James were old friends. They had gone to college together.

James had seen Dolley but had never met her. Burr told James that she was related to Patrick Henry. Even though Henry was not James's friend, James still wanted to meet Dolley.

Burr arranged a meeting between his two friends. James and Dolley got along very well, and soon—on September 15, 1793—they were married.

Many people in Dolley's family didn't agree with James's political ideas. James and Dolley didn't let that bother them. They would have a long and happy marriage.

A portrait of James Madison painted at the time he served as secretary of state under President Jefferson. James's job was to help the president decide how to deal with foreign countries.

"Mr. Madison's War"

I n 1796 Vice President John Adams was elected president. Thomas Jefferson, who had been secretary of state, received the second largest number of votes. He became vice president.

John Adams was a Federalist, and James was a Republican. He tired of fighting over ideas. He decided to retire and told friends that he was finished with politics.

But two years later, the **Alien** and **Sedition** Acts were passed by Congress. James just could not stand them. They allowed the government to put aliens, or people from other countries, in jail. All it took was for someone to think a foreigner was "dangerous to the peace and safety of the United States." The alien could even be kicked out of the country.

James didn't like that law. Someone could be called dangerous because they disagreed with the president. Good people could be put in prison just because of their ideas.

But one part of the law made James really angry. It said that anyone who criticized the government or a government official could be tried in court. This law went against the First Amendment of the Constitution. That amendment promises people freedom of speech, or the right to say what they want to say. James had worked hard to get that promise in the Constitution.

James was so upset that he decided to do something. He wrote resolutions adopted by the Virginia legislature to overrule the laws. Vice President Jefferson agreed and wrote similar resolutions for the Kentucky legislature.

Thomas Jefferson was an old friend of James's. When Jefferson was president, the two always worked well together.

John Adams only served one term as president. People were tired of the Federalist Party. In the elections of 1800, Thomas Jefferson beat Adams.

One of Jefferson's first acts as president was to make James Madison his secretary of state. The secretary of state gave advice about how the United States should deal with other countries.

James's job was difficult. The French leader Napoleon was trying to take over Europe. Both Britain and France were attacking American ships. Jefferson and James tried to protect the country's ships. They failed.

So Congress passed the **Embargo** Act of 1807. It stopped American ships from sailing to all foreign countries. This law was a disaster. Americans couldn't sell their products to other countries anymore. The lost sales hurt American businesses and some companies could not continue. People lost jobs and families had a hard time buying clothes and food.

Two years later, Congress decided the Embargo Act was a bad idea. Legislators replaced it with a new law that allowed trade with all countries except Britain and France. Life got a little better for families, but it was still hard.

By this time, Thomas Jefferson had been president for eight years. He chose not to run for president again. He told everyone that he wanted James Madison to be the next president. Some people wondered if Americans would want a president who had helped make life so hard for them.

The election of 1808 was not close. James won easily. Only 10 years before, he had talked about leaving politics. Now he was the president of the United States.

As soon as James took office, his wife Dolley got busy. She threw big parties and impressed everyone she met. She may have been better known on the streets of Washington than James was. The writer Washington Irving said, "Mrs. Madison . . . has a smile and a pleasant word for everybody."

Meanwhile James needed to solve the problems with Britain and France. The two countries kept stopping American ships. After Napoleon said the French wouldn't stop American ships anymore, James said it was all right to trade with them. But Napoleon had tricked James, and the French still stopped American ships.

This made American shippers along the East Coast very angry. They said the United States couldn't trust the French anymore.

The western states had their own problems. People heard rumors that the British were trying to get Native Americans to attack their towns. Then the Shawnee nation, led by Chief Tecumseh, tried to get other Indian nations to fight the Americans with them. They wanted to stop the white people from taking more of their land.

While Tecumseh was away getting more men to fight with him, William Henry Harrison and his troops attacked the Indian chief's headquarters, a Shawnee village by the Tippecanoe Creek, in Indiana. They destroyed it and killed many of the people who lived there. This attack is called the Battle of Tippecanoe. It started a long war with the Native Americans.

People living in the West learned about the battle. They were sure that the British were helping Tecumseh and his followers fight. They saw the British as their enemies.

James had a problem. People in the East didn't like the French. Those living in the West didn't like the British. All over the country, people were talking about starting a war against the British.

Some members of Congress also wanted to go to war. They believed America could beat Great Britain. But James felt that the United States wasn't ready and would lose a war. The navy was too weak.

People in New England were afraid a war would ruin their businesses. But the rest of the country was fed up with the actions of Great Britain. James had to make a hard decision. He talked with his old friend, Thomas Jefferson. He also asked his secretary of state, James Monroe, what he thought.

In November 1811, James decided that the country should go to war. After much more debate Congress agreed and on June 6, 1812, declared war on Great Britain.

New Englanders were against the war. They

called it "Mr. Madison's War." This was an election year and they decided they didn't want James to be president again. But the rest of the country liked James and he won the election easily. James would be president for four more years.

The war did not go well. The powerful British navy blocked American ships. It stopped anything from going into or out of the United States. The American navy tried to break the blockade, but it was too weak.

Then James became very sick. He thought he would die. Many people who disagreed with him hoped that he would. But James got better. Good news helped. In one naval battle, Oliver Perry defeated the British on Lake Erie. "We have met the enemy and they are ours," he reported.

The American army attacked British forces in Canada early in the war. The Americans were defeated and driven back. For two more years, the army attempted to take Canada. Neither side could win.

But in 1814, Britain defeated France. Troops

American ships defeat the British in a battle on Lake Erie during the War of 1812.

that had been fighting Napoleon were sent to Canada. All hopes for the United States taking over Canada ended. It looked as if Britain would win the war. And things got worse. On August 24, 1814, British troops entered Washington, D.C. It was the only time in history that a United States president was under enemy attack.

The British set fire to the Capitol, the White House, and several other public buildings. James and Dolley were forced to run from the city.

The British set fire to buildings in Washington, D.C. The White House burned, but Dolley Madison saved many important papers.

They were separated from each other for two days because of all the confusion. When Dolley escaped, she carried many important papers and kept them from being destroyed.

Three days later, James and Dolley returned to Washington. They were greeted with good news. The British had been defeated in Baltimore

Harbor. Francis Scott Key was being held prisoner on a British ship during that battle. As he watched the fighting, he wrote the words to "The Star-Spangled Banner."

The White House had burned to the ground, so the Madisons couldn't live there. They stayed in a private home near the White House, then moved to another house a short distance away.

The disaster in Washington was blamed on the secretary of war, John Armstrong. He hadn't made a good plan to defend the city from attack. James replaced him with Secretary of State Monroe. That gave Monroe two jobs in the president's cabinet.

People were horrified when they learned about Washington, D.C., being burned. The newspapers were full of reports about British victories and American defeats. Many voters blamed James for these events because he was the president.

To make matters worse, some people in the New England states were talking about breaking away from the United States. Things couldn't be worse for the country or for James.

But fortunately the British were tired of war. They had kept Canada from becoming part of the United States and didn't see any reason to keep fighting. Peace talks were held in Ghent, Belgium. And in December 1814, Britain and the United States signed the Treaty of Ghent, which ended the War of 1812.

Word of the peace treaty spread slowly. The fighting did not end. General Andrew Jackson and his men defeated the British in the Battle of New Orleans in early 1815. That victory and the peace treaty made James a popular president again. He became one of the most loved and respected men in the country. Once peace was established, Dolley began throwing parties for people in Washington.

People were proud to be Americans. After the war more people had jobs. They could afford to buy many things. New towns were settled in the West. People gave credit for all these things to James. He was happy to be liked after being so unpopular during the war.

The Battle of New Orleans, in which General Andrew Jackson and his men defeated the British. At the end of the war, James became a popular president.

James had been president for eight years. He said that he wanted his friend James Monroe to become the next president. People liked James Madison so much that most of them did what he asked. Monroe won the election easily. Most people agreed that making Monroe the next president was a way of showing how much they liked James.

A bust of James Madison is displayed in the state capitol in Richmond, Virginia. After leaving the White House, James continued to be interested in Virginia politics.

Life After the
White House

James Madison had finished his job. Upon leaving the White House, he and Dolley decided to leave Washington, D.C., too. They moved back to their plantation in Virginia.

Dolley had liked her busy life in Washington very much. Life on the plantation was awfully quiet by comparison. She still threw festive parties at Montpelier. However, the parties weren't nearly as big as they had been when James was president.

James's old friend Thomas Jefferson lived quite close by. Together they worked to found the

University of Virginia. They raised funds to build and run the school, made sure the builders did a good job, hired good teachers, and designed much of the college's **curriculum** themselves. This was a very busy and happy time for James and Thomas.

The two friends visited each other often. James had a favorite horse that Jefferson came to like very much. One day, Jefferson asked James if he could buy the horse from him. James said no. He was too attached to the horse to let him go.

His friend kept asking. At last, James agreed to sell his favorite horse. They settled on a price. A very happy Jefferson took the animal home with him. But a short time later, the horse got very sick and died. Jefferson had not yet paid for the horse. But he wanted to honor the bargain, and tried to pay James. James refused to take his friend's money.

They argued about it. Jefferson said that he owed the money because the horse was alive

**The University of Virginia was founded by James
and his friend Thomas Jefferson.**

when he took him home. James insisted the
horse had to have been sick already or it
would not have died so quickly. They finally
worked out their problem in a way that left
them both satisfied.

James loved the peacefulness of farming on his plantation. He experimented with many new farming methods. Many of these new ways of doing things had been developed by Jefferson.

During his eight years as president, James Monroe would often speak with James Madison and Thomas Jefferson. The president frequently asked them for their advice on various matters of national concern.

James had always been a good note taker. Over the years, he had carefully written down everything that was said and went on during the Constitutional Convention and all the other important meetings he had attended over the years. He always kept those notes.

After he moved back to Virginia, James organized all his notes of important meetings. He did the same thing with his papers and documents from his years in politics. James wanted them to be ready for publication after he died. Then people would have a history of how the United States began.

In 1826, Jefferson died. James was very sad to lose his best friend. He wanted the work that his friend had done to be remembered. So he organized all of Jefferson's important papers and letters so they could be published.

When he was 78 years old, James took part in a convention to write a new constitution for Virginia. As always, he said very little in public. Men argued a great deal about slavery. James wanted to make the state's slave owners less powerful than they were. He offered several ways of accomplishing this. But the men who wanted slavery were just too strong. All his ideas were voted down.

Soon after that, Madison's health began to decline. He stopped doing as much work in state and national affairs, but he never stopped reading. He had several newspapers sent to him, and he read them all.

Even as a boy, James had believed he would die young. He didn't. He died at his home on June 28, 1836, at the age of 85. He had been the

On May 24, 1844, Samuel F. B. Morse sent the first message on his invention, the telegraph. The message went from Washington, D.C., to Baltimore, Maryland.

It was a success that had taken years to achieve. He first thought of the invention in 1832, but gaining support and financing were difficult. Congress refused to give him a grant in 1838, but he asked again in 1843. This time he received $30,000 to test his invention.

Dolley Madison was very interested in the idea, and in 1844, she became the first to send a personal message over the telegraph.

last surviving member of the group that helped write the United States Constitution.

After James died, Dolley left the plantation. It was too quiet for her. She moved back to Washington, D.C., where many of her friends still lived. Dolley lived there for 13 more years until her death in 1849 at the age of 81. Despite the fact that the person who was closest to him was now gone as well, James Madison's legacy lived on. Today, he is celebrated as one of the United States' Founding Fathers.

GLOSSARY

alien–a person from another country

alliance–an arrangement by which countries agree to work together because of a shared need

ally–a nation who has agreed to help another nation

amendment–a change made to the Constitution

avid–very eager

cabinet–a committee of advisors or ministers serving a president or other head of state

campaigning–to carry out a series of meetings and events with the goal of winning an election

constitution–the basic laws of a state or nation

curriculum–an outline of what subjects will be taught at school

embargo–a government order forbidding ships from entering or leaving its ports

epilepsy–a disorder of the nervous system; a person with epilepsy may pass out or have convulsions

inalienable rights–guaranteed freedoms of citizens

inauguration–a ceremony during which a person is officially put in office

legislature–a body of lawmakers

levy–to impose by legal authority

militia–an army of citizens who are not regular soldiers

navigation–the act of sailing or steering a ship

pen name–a made-up name used by writers instead of their
real name

precedent–an action that serves as a model for later actions

ratify–to approve officially

sedition–speech or action causing rebellion against the
government

theology–the study of God and of how God relates to the
world

CHRONOLOGY

1751 Born in Port Conway, Virginia, on March 16.

1769 Enters the College of New Jersey (now Princeton University).

1771 Graduates from college.

1774 Elected to serve on the Orange County (VA) Committee of Safety.

1776 The Declaration of Independence is signed; elected representative from Orange County to the Virginia State Convention.

1779 Elected to the Continental Congress.

1784 Elected to the Virginia House of Delegates.

1787 Serves at the Constitutional Congress.

1788 The new Constitution is ratified.

1789 Elected to the House of Representatives.

1793 Marries Dolley Payne Todd on September 15.

1801 Appointed secretary of state.

1808 Elected as the fourth president of the United States.

1812 War is declared on Britain; reelected president of the United States.

1814 Washington, D.C., is burned by the British; the Treaty of Ghent is signed, ending the war with Britain.

1817 Leaves office when term ends; returns to family plantation.

1829 Serves at the Virginia Constitutional Convention.

1836 Dies at home on June 28.

REVOLUTIONARY WAR TIME LINE

1765   The Stamp Act is passed by the British. Violent protests against it break out in the colonies.

1766   Britain ends the Stamp Act.

1767   Britain passes a law that taxes glass, painter's lead, paper, and tea in the colonies.

1770   Five colonists are killed by British soldiers in the Boston Massacre.

1773   People are angry about the taxes on tea. They throw boxes of tea from ships in Boston Harbor into the water. It ruins the tea. The event is called the Boston Tea Party.

1774   The British pass laws to punish Boston for the Boston Tea Party. They close Boston Harbor. Leaders in the colonies meet to plan a response to these actions.

1775   The Battles of Lexington and Concord begin the American Revolution.

1776   The Declaration of Independence is signed. France and Spain give money to help the Americans fight Britain. Nathan Hale is captured by the British. He is charged with being a spy and is executed.

1777   Leaders choose a flag for America. The American troops win some important battles over the British. General Washington and his troops spend a very cold, hungry winter in Valley Forge.

1778 France sends ships to help the Americans win the war. The British are forced to leave Philadelphia.

1779 French ships head back to France. The French support the Americans in other ways.

1780 Americans discover that Benedict Arnold is a traitor. He escapes to the British. Major battles take place in North and South Carolina.

1781 The British surrender at Yorktown.

1783 A peace treaty is signed in France. British troops leave New York.

1787 The U.S. Constitution is written. Delaware becomes the first state in the Union.

1789 George Washington becomes the first president. John Adams is vice president.

FURTHER READING

Clinton, Susan. *James Madison: Fourth President of the United States*. Danbury, Conn.: Children's Press, 1987.

Davidson, Mary R. *Dolly Madison: Famous First Lady*. Philadelphia: Chelsea House, 1992.

Fritz, Jean. *The Great Little Madison*. New York: Putnam and Grosset, 1989.

Isaacs, Sally Senzell. *America in the Time of George Washington*. Portsmouth, N.H.: Heinemann, 1998.

Malone, Mary. *James Madison*. Berkeley Heights, N.J.: Enslow, 1997.

INDEX

PICTURE CREDITS

ABOUT THE AUTHOR

BRENT KELLEY is a veterinarian and writer. He is the author of many books on baseball history. Two books (using the pen name Grant Kendall) tell about his experiences as a veterinarian. He has also written two books for Chelsea House. He is a columnist for *Thoroughbred Times,* a weekly horse racing and breeding publication. He also writes for *Bourbon Times,* a weekly family newspaper. He has written nearly 400 articles for magazines and newspapers. He lives in Paris, Kentucky, with his wife and children.

Senior Consulting Editor **ARTHUR M. SCHLESINGER, JR.** is the leading American historian of our time. He won the Pulitzer Prize for his book *The Age of Jackson* (1945), and again for *A Thousand Days* (1965). This chronicle of the Kennedy Administration also won a National Book Award. He has written many other books, including a multi-volume series, *The Age of Roosevelt.* Professor Schlesinger is the Albert Schweitzer Professor of the Humanities at the City University of New York, and has been involved in several other Chelsea House projects, including the COLONIAL LEADERS series of biographies on the most prominent figures of early American history.